101
ESSENTIAL TIPS

Training Your
DOG

ESSENTIAL 101 TIPS

Training Your

DOG

Bruce Fogle, DVM

Training sequences by Patricia Holden White

A DK PUBLISHING BOOK

Editor Damien Moore
Art Editor Claire Pegrum
Series Editor Gillian Roberts
Series Art Editor Clive Hayball
Production Controller Lauren Britton
US Editor Laaren Brown

First American Edition, 1997
2 4 6 8 10 9 7 5 3 1
Published in the United States by DK Publishing, Inc.
95 Madison Avenue, New York, New York 10016

Visit us on the World Wide Web at http://www.dk.com

A catalog record is available from the Library of Congress

ISBN 0-7894-1460-0

Text film output by The Right Type, Great Britain
Reproduced by Colourscan, Singapore
Printed and bound in Italy by Graphicom

ESSENTIAL TIPS

101

UNDERSTANDING YOUR DOG

1 THE RIGHT DOG FOR YOU

It is important to select a dog carefully, according to your interests, your lifestyle, and your current and future circumstances. Consider the difference between raising a dog from a puppy, which will require patient house training, or acquiring a full-grown dog, perhaps complete with hidden behavioral problems. Think, also, about the implications of the dog's size and sex, and find out how much exercise it will need.

Dense coat sheds profusely

SMALL BUT TOUGH
The smallest of all dog breeds, Chihuahuas are surprisingly robust and active dogs.

GENTLE GIANT
The giant Newfoundland will present you with an equally gigantic food bill.

2 SOURCES OF DOGS

Recognized breeders, friends and neighbors, and animal rescue centers can all be good sources of dogs. Breeding establishments that sell dogs primarily as a business are likely to be less reliable than breeders affiliated with registered breed clubs.

- Good dog shelters will always interview prospective owners.
- Generally, don't buy puppies from pet shops.

ASK FOR MOTHER
When buying a pup, ask to see the mother to get an idea of the pup's potential temperament.

3 WHICH SEX?

Consider the benefits or drawbacks of either sex, as well as the pros and cons of neutered dogs. Neutered dogs and females are the easiest to train; unneutered males are the least responsive. Males are often bigger and exhibit the typically masculine traits of being territorial and dominant.

Female has smaller head than male

TOP DOG
Because he is male, the darker Golden Retriever is larger than the female.

4 BREED CHARACTERISTICS

By choosing a pedigree dog, you know in advance its potential size, and its grooming, feeding, and exercise requirements. You will even know its life expectancy. Specific breeds are associated with certain aspects of behavior, and some types of dogs are more predisposed toward training than others. It is a good idea to choose the breed that is most suited to your own needs, temperament, and lifestyle.

TERRIERS ▷
Originally developed to chase small game and vermin, most terriers are lively and robust; but they are the breeds most likely to snap or nip.

Small, pointed ears

Dense topcoat with furry undercoat

Sturdy body

THE WOLF WITHIN
Through selective breeding, humans have accentuated certain wolf characteristics and diminished others. But, remember, regardless of its size or conformation, your dog is a domesticated wolf.

Tail left undocked

Deep chest indicates active temperament

Coat is sleek, smooth, and short

◁ GUNDOGS
Setters, retrievers, pointers, and spaniels were bred to respond to human commands. As a result, they are often loyal and responsive.

Tail is docked
for fashion

Strong, slightly
arched neck

◁ **GUARD DOGS**
Acquire this type
of dog only if you
have ample dog-
handling experience.
A large dog can be
difficult to control
without proper
obedience training.

Shiny, flat
topcoat requires
little grooming

Legs have
plenty of
thick bone

HERDING DOGS ▷
Herding dogs evolved to work
as teams with shepherds
and farmers. They are
loyal and energetic,
but they bark
when excited
and tend
to nip.

Dense, soft
topcoat

Coat needs to be
groomed regularly

◁ **COMPANION DOGS**
Toy dogs have been bred especially
for companionship. They thrive on
affection and human contact. Despite
their diminutive stature, toy dogs can
make highly effective burglar alarms.

11

5 DOMINANT DOGS

Although each breed of dog has its own general personality profile (*Tip 4*), ultimately every dog is unique. Some dogs have naturally dominant personalities; other dogs are submissive. Both types of dog can be well trained, but a dominant dog is most likely to resist obeying commands. More dominant dogs require firm handling.

◁ EYE TO EYE
Two confident dogs attempt to outstare each other. The dog that wins this battle of nerves will exert rank seniority. Size is not necessarily a factor.

DON'T TAKE RISKS
If you feel at all concerned about the behavior of your dominant dog, contact your local training club and arrange one-to-one or group obedience lessons.

DOMINANT TRAITS ▽
With ears and tail held erect, this dominant German Shepherd advances boldly. The Dalmatian offers no challenge.

Dalmatian backs off submissively

6 SUBMISSIVE DOGS

Do not issue commands too harshly when you are training a submissive or insecure dog – a slow and gentle approach is required. Submissive dogs can be overwhelmed when commanded to obey and will respond by cowering or rolling over.

COWERING COLLIE
Overwhelmed by a harsh command, this intensely submissive Collie rolls over and tucks its tail between its legs. Note how it turns its head away to avoid eye contact.

7 LEADER OF THE PACK

In all relationships with dogs, the human must play the part of "top dog." Few dogs want to be pack leaders. The vast majority feel secure knowing that there is someone in command. Early obedience training reinforces this natural canine behavior and teaches puppies to respond to human commands.

Child plays gently with pet dog

FAMILY FRIEND
This German Shepherd is happy to obey all members of its surrogate family.

EARLY LEARNING

8 INITIAL INFLUENCES

The period from birth to three months of age is the most important in a dog's life. This is the time when it learns about itself, its littermates, and the world around it. It discovers what is fun and what is dangerous. The more a young dog is allowed to investigate its surroundings, the more developed its brain becomes. A happy, alert pup is easier to train.

Head can be lifted

△ **SEVEN DAYS**
During the first week of its life, the pup is both blind and deaf. It employs heat sensors in its nose to locate its mother.

Puppy moves around tentatively

△ **FOURTEEN DAYS**
After two weeks, the pup's eyes are open. Using all four legs, it can now just raise itself off the ground.

Movement is now deliberate and coordinated

△ **THREE WEEKS**
The puppy now has the ability to move around in the direction of its choice.

SIX WEEKS ▷
The confident pup is now ready to investigate the world around it.

9 MEETING PEOPLE

Make sure your pup meets as many people as possible while it is still very young. Ask friends to kneel down and greet the pup to help curb its inclination to jump up. Advise your friends to avoid direct eye contact, which often provokes an unduly excited response. Reward calm behavior with a food treat.

ENJOYING COMPANY
Take your pup to visit your friends' homes whenever possible.

10 MEETING OTHER ANIMALS

Whenever possible, introduce your pup to other species that it is likely to encounter. It is best to do this when the dog is less than 12 weeks old. After that age, greater care must be taken to make sure that neither its natural predatory instincts nor its fear of strange animals is stimulated.
Always supervise meetings.

KILLER INSTINCT
For thousands of years of evolution, dogs survived by killing animals. This instinct still remains intense in some breeds.

Cat confidently holds its ground

DOGS & CATS
By making friends with a cat at an early age, this young pup is less likely to chase cats when it is fully grown.

FREE-FOR-ALL
Playfights are the most popular pastime at puppy parties.

11 PUPPY PARTIES

With the permission of your vet or local dog-training club, organize or participate in supervised weekly puppy meetings. At these informal gatherings, puppies will soon learn how to behave around other dogs and strangers.

Submissive puppy rolls over

Tail wags indicating contentment

12 CONSTRUCTIVE FUN

Set aside time each day to offer your puppy some stimulating indoor physical and mental activity. Nurturing the bond between you and your dog through constructive play is not only enjoyable, it also helps reinforce basic obedience. When the pup obeys a command, give an immediate reward such as stroking or encouraging words.

TUG-OF-WAR
Stay in control: do not encourage your dog to nip.

13 DON'T ENCOURAGE BAD HABITS

Reinforce only good behavior. You may find certain traits, such as begging for food and pawing for attention, endearing in a pup, but these habits become unacceptable when your dog is fully grown. So resist the temptation to encourage such behavior.

SPOILING YOUR PUPPY
If you carry a puppy constantly when it is young, it will expect the same treatment if it feels insecure as an adult.

14 FEARS & PHOBIAS

Oversee all of your puppy's activities to make sure that frightening situations are kept to a minimum. Fears that are learned at an early age can develop into enduring phobias unless overcome rapidly.

ONCE BITTEN
A puppy that has been bitten may develop canine phobia – a lifelong fear of dogs.

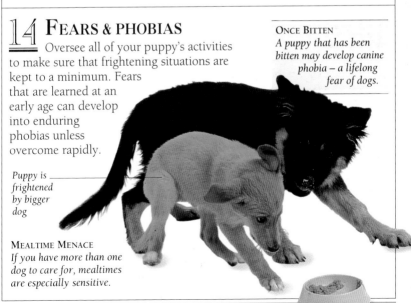

Puppy is frightened by bigger dog

MEALTIME MENACE
If you have more than one dog to care for, mealtimes are especially sensitive.

REWARDS & DISCIPLINE

15 GIVING PRAISE

Dogs need constant encouragement when they are being trained. Food snacks, toys, and physical contact and verbal praise from their owners are all strong rewards. Every time your dog obeys a command, praise it to let it know that you are pleased. Your dog will soon understand simple praise like "good dog."

HANDLING A PUP
The earlier a dog is accustomed to being handled by people, the better.

Stroke along side of dog's body

STROKING YOUR DOG
Give your dog long strokes along the side of its body. Stroking is comforting to the dog and shows that you are in control.

16 THE IMPORTANCE OF TOYS

Puppies chew objects in order to learn about their environment. By providing a dog with toys, you can make sure that, even in your absence, your dog can stimulate its mind and senses without resorting to destructive behavior.

Chewing strengthens puppy's jaws

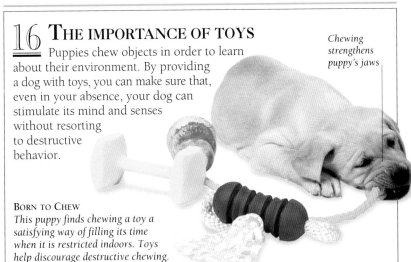

BORN TO CHEW
This puppy finds chewing a toy a satisfying way of filling its time when it is restricted indoors. Toys help discourage destructive chewing.

17 REWARDING TOYS

The best toys have their own unique smells and are unlike any other thing that the dog might find. Balls and Frisbees are excellent for chasing, catching, and retrieving; bones are more satisfying to chew.

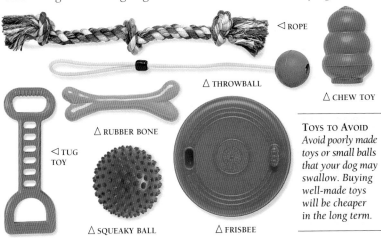

△ ROPE

△ THROWBALL

△ CHEW TOY

△ RUBBER BONE

◁ TUG TOY

△ SQUEAKY BALL

△ FRISBEE

TOYS TO AVOID
Avoid poorly made toys or small balls that your dog may swallow. Buying well-made toys will be cheaper in the long term.

18 TOO MANY TOYS

Train your dog to chew its own toys to discourage it from damaging household goods. If a dog is given too many toys, it may think that it can chew anything. Allow a maximum of three toys that are not like any other household item. Don't give your dog old clothes or shoes to play with. If your dog is allowed to chew these items, it will assume that it may chew any other articles of clothing. Dogs cannot distinguish between old items and new ones.

19 CHOOSING TREATS

Find out which snacks your dog likes best and give these special treats as rewards for good behavior. However, don't overstimulate your dog by using too many food treats, and never give your dog sweets.

△ MIXED ASSORTMENT   △ BACON TREATS   △ MARROW-BONE

20 UNPLANNED REWARDS

Scavenging for tidbits can become a habit if rewarded, albeit unintentionally, with success. Stop this problem from developing by securing all trash and keeping tempting items out of reach. In its quest for food items, your dog may swallow damaging inedible objects.

RAID!
This single-minded male Labrador finds a full trash can an irresistible temptation.

Labrador Retrievers are notorious scavengers

21 CORRECT DISCIPLINE

Never use physical punishment to discipline your dog. Instead, give it an unpleasant surprise as soon as you see it misbehaving. A small squirt from a water pistol or spray gun will do the trick, or a blast from a high-pitched alarm.

◁ ALARM

△ WATER PISTOL

△ SPRAY GUN

22 GOOD TIMING

Reprimand your dog only when you actually observe it being disobedient. Displaying anger after the event will just confuse the dog, because it will not understand why you are angry. Inappropriate and poorly timed disciplinary action will undermine your correct disciplinary tactics. You can learn to anticipate your dog's behavior by observing its body language.

A FAIR COP
Caught in the act of destroying some clothing, this dog is likely to understand the reason why it is disciplined by its owner.

Owner catches dog destroying clothing

Dog responds to owner's reprimand

23 REDUCING REWARDS

Initially, it will be most effective to combine food rewards (*Tip 19*) with verbal praise. After a while, however, gradually reduce the amount of food rewards while continuing to give either physical or verbal praise. The dog will soon learn to respond to verbal praise alone. Note that small breeds are often more selective eaters than large ones, so they may not respond well to food rewards at any stage.

TRAINING TACTICS

24 MAKE LEARNING FUN

Daily training sessions should always be enjoyable occasions for both you and your dog.
- Do not attempt to train if either one of you isn't concentrating; a dog will know if you are bored.
- Always finish with something the dog enjoys and is able to do. However, don't save the best rewards for the end – the dog may want to finish the exercise quickly to receive its final reward.

WILLING WORKER
A dog enjoys nothing more than pleasing you – its surrogate pack leader.

SOCIAL RESPONSIBILITY
Dogs are social animals. Your dog relies on you to train it to be trusting, even-tempered, and sociable.

Dog retrieves favorite toy

Stance is alert and confident

Owner kneels to praise dog

25 WHEN TO TRAIN

It is best to train when your dog is hungry. It will be mentally alert and will respond more readily to food rewards. Note that dogs have much shorter attention spans than humans, so keep the sessions short. Train for a maximum of 15 minutes, twice a day. Giving a dog two meals a day will create time for two good training sessions.

HUNGRY FOR KNOWLEDGE
Golden Retrievers have excellent appetites. Food rewards go down well with the majority of dogs.

SMALL APPETITES
Small breeds are usually more selective eaters than large ones, so they do not necessarily respond well to food rewards.

26 THE RIGHT ENVIRONMENT

Begin training in the quiet environment of your home. Once the dog reliably obeys your commands, move to a quiet location outdoors and repeat the training sessions. Once your dog is obedient both indoors and in quiet outdoor locations, graduate to a busier area. Be sure to vary the places in which you train your dog, so that you maintain its interest.

OUTDOOR LOCATION

27 GIVING COMMANDS

Dogs have a limited ability to understand the human language and respond best to short, sharp commands. Attract your dog's attention by speaking its name, then give your command.

- The inflection of your voice is important when giving commands. Lower the tone of your voice to reprimand your dog; use a higher tone for praise.
- Avoid constantly repeating a command: this will only confuse your dog.

Hand signals reinforce verbal commands

FULL ATTENTION
This German Shepherd is attentive and alert to its owner's commands.

28 BODY LANGUAGE

Dogs are adept at reading human body language. Encourage your dog to respond to you by assuming a welcoming posture. Be enthusiastic and generous with your praise, and dramatic when you reprimand your dog. Smile when you are pleased, and grimace if the dog willfully disobeys your command.

ENTHUSIASTIC GREETING
Here, the owner praises her obedient dog by smiling and giving positive, dramatic body signals.

Owner greets dog with open arms

Dog comes and wags its tail confidently

29 ENFORCING COMMANDS

Make sure that you are always in a position of control so that you are able to enforce your commands. This is particularly important during outdoor training sessions, where the dog may be a danger to itself and others if it does not obey commands reliably. So, keep your dog on a long training leash during all training sessions until you are confident of being in control.

FIRMLY IN CONTROL
By standing upright with shoulders back, this trainer keeps the dog's attention. The leash enables her to enforce commands.

DON'T CHASE YOUR DOG
If your dog pulls the leash out of your hand, call it back firmly or use a food lure. Chasing will be seen as a game.

30 TRAINING IS NOT EXERCISE

Dogs need plenty of regular exercise, as well as time to play with other dogs. Training is not a substitute for either of these, so be sure that your dog gets the exercise its age, breed, and temperament require.

A game of "chase" is fun exercise

31 THE VALUE OF SAYING "NO"

"No" is one of the most important words your dog will learn. With this one command, you can regain control or prevent your dog from doing something dangerous. The timing of your commands (*Tip 22*) and knowing when to say "No" are important elements of dog training. If, for example, a nervous dog backs away from a stranger, and you try to reassure it by saying "it's okay," you are actually telling the dog that you approve of its behavior. Instead, say "No" firmly, adopting a stern tone and a dominant stance.

TRAINING EQUIPMENT

32 CHOOSING ACCESSORIES

Be sure to choose accessories that are appropriate for the size and temperament of your dog. You will need a long leash for training, as well as the standard walking leash.

- Bean bags make ideal beds, and newspaper-lined playpens provide for controlled house training.
- Remember to replace your dog's collar frequently as it grows.

COLLARS
Always choose the right length of collar for the dog's neck.

△ DESIGNER COLLAR

△ NYLON COLLAR

△ LEATHER COLLAR

△ BRAIDED LEATHER LEASH

CHOICE OF LEASHES
Leashes are usually made of leather, rope, or nylon. Braided leather is comfortable and long lasting.

◁ **COTTON LEASH**
Use a long cotton leash such as this for keeping control of your dog outdoors and for reinforcing your commands.

EXTENSION LEASH ▷
This type of leash allows your dog greater freedom of movement.

△ BASKET
MUZZLE

△ HARNESS

CONTROL DEVICES
A harness avoids pressure on the dog's neck if it pulls. A muzzle is useful for preventing destructive dogs from chewing.

BEAN-BAG BED ▷
With washable covers, bean bags make ideal beds.

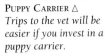

PUPPY CARRIER △
Trips to the vet will be easier if you invest in a puppy carrier.

PUPPY CRATE ▷
A crate makes a good den for your dog – and a much easier life for you when traveling with your dog.

Dog is happy alone with its toy

27

33 MORE LEASHES

In addition to a standard leash, you will require a long cotton leash for outdoor training, and an equally long houseline with a bolt snap for indoor control. Make sure that the leash and bolt snap are not too heavy for your dog. Extension leashes are a practical choice, since they allow your dog some freedom while you still maintain control.

▽ NYLON CORD HOUSELINE

◁ TRAINING LONGLINE

34 COLLAR YOUR DOG

Simple buckle collars are the best choice for most dogs. Attach an ID tag or container with a contact telephone number inside in case your dog strays. Half-choke collars are ideal for boisterous dogs with short attention spans. Choke chains are useful when they are used properly, but they should never be used on breeds with delicate windpipes such as Yorkshire Terriers.

△ ID TAG

CORRECT FIT
While your dog is growing up, keep a check on the fit of its collar. You should be able to slip two fingers under the collar.

◁ ID CONTAINER

△ CHOKE CHAIN

△ HALF-CHOKE COLLAR

35 FITTING A HALF-CHOKE COLLAR

Fit a half-choke collar so that the soft webbing lies around your dog's throat, while the chain links sit at the back of the neck.

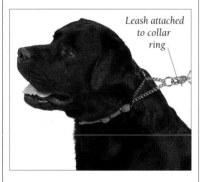

Leash attached to collar ring

36 HEAD HALTER

Use a head halter to control large, independent dogs. Clip the leash onto the halter: if the dog lunges, its own momentum pulls its jaws shut and its head down.

Halter fastens behind neck

37 HARNESSING YOUR DOG

A small dog is often more comfortable wearing a harness than it would be with other forms of restraint. It slips over the dog's body and around the chest, so avoiding collar pressure on the neck if the dog pulls on its leash.

DOG IN HARNESS
Remember to buy the right size harness for your dog.

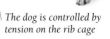

Leash attaches to backstrap of harness

SPACE TO BREATHE
A light harness is suitable for small dogs with soft windpipes, such as Yorkshire Terriers and Chihuahuas, and for those with muscular necks, such as Pugs.

The dog is controlled by tension on the rib cage

INDOOR TRAINING

38 EARLY HOME ROUTINES

All family members should handle a puppy while it learns to wear a collar and leash, eat from its own bowl, sleep in its own bed, and come when called. But one person should be primarily responsible for training.

Dog enjoys human contact

BUILDING A FRIENDSHIP
Routine training establishes a strong bond between you and your pet dog.

39 PERSONAL SPACE FOR YOUR DOG

Do not isolate new canine family members: dogs are sociable animals. Set up a bed as a personal space for your dog, and place it in a busy area of the home, such as a corner of the kitchen. Like its ancestor the wolf, your pet dog likes to enjoy the security of its own personal space, which is the equivalent of a wolf's den.

40 NO NIPPING

Discipline your puppy each time it nips you by saying "No" firmly. If the puppy persists despite this admonition, you can grab it by the scruff of the neck firmly but without causing pain, mimicking the way in which the puppy's mother would have administered discipline.

NIP IT IN THE BUD
Biting is a natural part of puppy play, but it must never be encouraged by you or other family members.

41 PUPPY CRATES

To a dog that has been trained from puppyhood to use it, a crate becomes its own secure haven. Crate training encourages house training, reduces destructive behavior, and eases traveling with your dog. Place soft bedding, a bowl of water, and your puppy's favorite toy inside the crate.

DEN NOT DUNGEON
A crate should be a pleasant place for your dog: never use it for disciplinary purposes.

PUPPY PLAYPEN
Although this puppy is happy to play in its crate, it should not be confined for more than two hours at any time during the day.

42 HOUSE TRAINING

Your puppy will want to eliminate after it wakes up, eats, or plays. As it sniffs the ground – a sign that it is about to eliminate – take it to the place you have chosen for it to relieve itself and say "Hurry up." Before long, your dog will eliminate when you give the "Hurry up" command.

Puppy urinates on newspaper

PAPER TRAINING
Place the pup in an area covered with newspaper, and praise it when it relieves itself. Say "No" firmly if it attempts to urinate off the paper.

43 MOVING OUTSIDE

Start outdoor training alongside house training as soon as possible. Take a small piece of soiled paper with you; the puppy will smell its own scent and be encouraged to transfer toileting outside. When taking your dog to a public place, remember to carry a specially made "pooper scooper" with you, or a simple plastic bag, and be sure to clean up after your dog.

SCOOPING POOP

44 GROOM YOUR DOG

Brush designed for long coats

Grooming your dog daily not only keeps it clean and healthy but also helps to reassert your authority over it. Picking up the dog, holding its head, and opening its mouth are dominant gestures that reinforce your control. Initially, use food rewards as distractions throughout the grooming session.

45 THREE ESSENTIAL COMMANDS

The "Come," "Sit," and "Stay" commands are the most important lessons that you can teach your dog, since they enable you to keep it under control at all times. All dog owners have the responsibility for ensuring that their pets are not a nuisance. Be sure to praise the dog when it responds well. When it disobeys a command, repeat the exercise from the previous level of success.

46 COMING TO YOU

Train your puppy to come to you on command when it is alert and hungry. Divide its meal into ten portions, and throughout the day entice it to the food bowl, using its name and the command "Come." As the puppy comes to you, kneel down and praise it by saying "Good dog" with enthusiasm, and give the food.

TOY REWARD
You can use a toy to entice the puppy.

Long training leash

47 THE "SIT" COMMAND

Once your puppy responds well to the command to come (*Tip 46*), teach it to sit. Call the puppy to you, showing it a food treat. As it reaches you, move the treat slowly up and over its head. The pup will naturally sit down in order to keep its eye on the food. Give the command "Sit" when you see the puppy begin to bend its hind legs. Initially, reward each response with verbal praise and treats.

Owner holds treat in right hand

STAY CALM
Keep the leash in your left hand and a food treat in the right. It is important to be calm and not to excite the puppy.

REFUSING TO SIT
If the puppy will not sit for a food reward, kneel down and hold its collar with one hand, tucking its hind quarters under with the other hand. Give the command "Sit" as you do this, then praise it.

48 LEARNING THE "DOWN" COMMAND

Train your dog to lie down reliably on your command before moving outdoors where there are dangers such as busy roads. There are two lying down positions – "sphinx," in which the hind legs are tucked under, and "flat," where the hips are rolled and the legs are to one side. At this stage, it doesn't matter which position it assumes.

1 ◁ Command the pup to sit, and kneel down beside it. Hold the collar in one hand, and place a tasty treat by its nose. If the pup tries to get up, tuck its hindquarters under and say "Sit."

Hold collar in right hand

Leash is secured under knee to maintain control

RELUCTANT LIES
If your dog does not stay down, press gently over its shoulders. After a few seconds, release the puppy, saying "okay."

2 △ Without releasing the collar, move the treat forward and down: the pup will follow with its nose. As the pup starts to lie down, give it the command "Down."

3 ◁ As soon as the pup lies down, reward it with the treat and praise. Be careful not to praise excessively, since this will encourage your puppy to jump up.

49 WALKING WITHOUT A LEASH

It is often easiest to train a puppy to walk to heel off the leash at first, since it will enjoy human companionship and will usually be willing to follow its owner. Using the scent of food to attract the puppy, give the command "Heel." Be ready to grasp the collar if the puppy wanders, and attempt to cover only small distances initially.

Owner kneels beside puppy

1 ◁ Kneel to the right of your alert seated puppy. Holding its collar with your left hand, speak its name, and show it a favorite treat in your right hand.

Owner bends to discourage jumping up

Leash is visible over shoulder

Puppy eager to follow food

2 △ Walking forward, give the command "Heel." Then, turn right, drawing the treat around with you. Repeat the command.

3 ◁ To turn left, hold the collar with your left hand and command "Steady." Place the reward close to your dog's mouth, then move it to the left. The puppy will follow.

50 WALKING ON A LEASH

Make sure that walking your dog is always a pleasure rather than a chore by teaching it from an early age to walk to heel on its leash. Start training indoors, using a long training leash. Let the puppy look at and smell the leash. Then attach the leash to the puppy's comfortable, well-fitting collar.

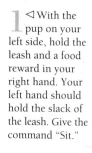

1 ◁ With the pup on your left side, hold the leash and a food reward in your right hand. Your left hand should hold the slack of the leash. Give the command "Sit."

Puppy is alert

Owner gives command "Heel"

Give leash a light jerk

2 ◁ Move forward on your left foot and command the pup to "Heel." If the pup strays too far ahead, give the leash a quick, light jerk to pull it back.

Maintain eye contact

LEASHES ARE FOR FUN
Your dog should always associate the sight of its leash with pleasurable activities. Never use a leash to punish a dog.

3 ▷ With the puppy beside you in the heel position, offer it the food reward and say "Good dog." Repeat the "Sit" command, and praise your puppy when it obeys.

Puppy follows scent of treat

4 △ After the dog has learned to walk to heel in a straight line, teach it to turn right by guiding it with a treat.

5 △ To turn left, increase your own speed and hold a treat in front of the puppy's nose to slow it down.

51 PREVENT PULLING

Do not allow your dog to pull on its leash. As well as being uncomfortable for you, it can make the dog overexcited (*Tip 90*) and may be intimidating to other people. Try giving a quick, light jerk on the leash as the dog pulls forward. If this does not work, command the puppy to sit each time it pulls. Neither you nor the puppy should lose concentration, and you should not shout the commands. Use a head halter on boisterous dogs.

Hand pulls back once, gently but firmly

FIRM HANDLING
When the dog pulls, slide your left hand down the leash and pull back firmly. Give the command "Sit." Start to walk again, giving the command "Heel."

Owner is pulled forward by dog

52 LEARNING TO IGNORE DISTRACTIONS

Even the most obedient dog may lapse when faced with a tantalizing diversion. After training your dog to come on command (*Tip 46*), offer an enticing distraction such as a succulent bone. As your dog lunges forward, give the command "Leave." Reinforce the command with a gentle jerk on the leash. Use an extendable leash until your dog responds willingly.

SWEET TEMPTATION
Distracted by a tasty morsel, this German Shepherd ignores its owner.

TEST OF WILL
Pulling on the leash may be a manifestation of a dog's dominant nature. Such dogs are likely to need remedial training.

53 LEASH CHEWING

To young and boisterous dogs, leashes are exciting new toys. Such dogs will often chew their leashes, or try to climb them. If your dog persistently chews its leash, spray the leash with a special bitter-tasting liquid, which can be purchased at most pet shops or veterinary offices. As its name suggests, this nontoxic bitter spray makes the leash unpleasant to taste. When the dog chews the leash, it is disciplined by the nasty taste, rather than by you.

LEASH TIPS
Don't use the dog's leash to play tug-of-war games. And be sure to store the leash out of reach after your walks.

BITTER SPRAY

54 "SIT" & "STAY"

The commands "Sit" and "Stay" form the basis of responsible pet ownership and are useful forms of control during outdoor activity. Begin this training exercise in a quiet indoor area, such as a hallway, and limit each session to 15 minutes. If the dog moves, hold it by the collar with your left hand and tuck its bottom down with your right. Do not expect the dog to understand the commands immediately.

1 ▷ Show a treat in your right hand. As the dog sits to concentrate on the food, say "Sit."

2 ▷ Maintain a gentle tension on the leash and step forward with your right foot. Give the command "Stay."

3 ◁ Reward the dog for staying. Now slowly walk around the dog, holding the leash above its head. You should not need to repeat the command.

Dog senses contact through taut leash

4 ▷ After a few sessions, the dog should sit and stay while on the leash. Now drop the leash and repeat the steps, praising the dog's good behavior.

Dog awaits owner's command

OUTDOOR TRAINING

55 RESPONSIBLE OWNERSHIP

Remember that enjoying the love, loyalty, and companionship of a canine brings obligations to maintain not only the dog's basic needs but also the quality of life of your family, friends, and neighbors. Be sure to obey the local legal requirements concerning dogs, and you may want to obtain insurance for your dog.

DANGEROUS DOGS
Following public concern, it is now an offense in many areas to allow a dog to be dangerously out of control in a public place. Your vet can advise you on local regulations.

CONTROL YOUR DOG
Some dogs are more powerful than their owners and require firm handling.

SAFETY FIRST

56 ROAD SENSE

Once your puppy responds to commands in your home and yard, you can move to busier environments. With the approval of your vet, take your dog to public places so that it can become accustomed to traffic noise. Use a leash to keep your dog safe and under control at all times. Always command your dog to sit before crossing a road.

57 INTRODUCING THE CAR

Train your dog to look upon the car as a second home. Dogs can quite naturally enjoy car journeys, both because they find the trips exciting, and because car journeys often end in exercise and meeting with other dogs. Take your dog on frequent short trips so that it becomes accustomed to the car. If your dog experiences car sickness, do not feed it before the trip, and protect the car with newspaper.

Encourage dog using a food treat

Dog approaches confidently

CARS CAN KILL
Never leave your dog unattended in a car in warm weather. Dogs can suffer from fatal heatstroke as a result of overheating. Even parking in the shade is not safe.

1 △ Before setting out, entice the dog into your parked car with a food reward or a toy. Once the dog is happy to sit in the car, accustom it to the sound of the engine.

2 ▷ Give food rewards and verbal praise when the dog displays no signs of agitation. Go for short drives at first and gradually increase their duration.

58 CONTROL & RESTRAINT

Always keep your dog under control when taking it out to a public place.

- Muzzle your dog if you have any doubts about its temperament, especially in the presence of children.
- Use only a safe, basket-type muzzle that allows the dog to pant freely (*Tip 32*).

USING A MUZZLE
A comfortable muzzle that fits well is no hardship to a dog. This Golden Retriever wears a muzzle to prevent scavenging.

CONTROL WITH KIDS
A dog should always wear a muzzle in the presence of toddlers. This is particularly important if the dog has been trained to guard or chase.

59 THE IMPORTANCE OF PLAYTIME

Socialize your pet by arranging meetings with dogs that are well controlled. Keep both dogs on their leashes for the initial introduction. After they have sniffed each other thoroughly and become acquainted, allow them to play together. It is through play that dogs learn about each other, and it helps cement their pack relationships.

Nibbling is just play

PLAY FIGHT
In simple play, dogs try to mouth each other or gently chew the head region. They may growl and bark theatrically.

60 DOGS WITH CHILDREN

Even the friendliest dog should be introduced to young children only in the presence, and under the supervision, of an adult. While a dog may enjoy being petted by adults, it might not be used to the more rapid and jerky movements of children.

- Instruct children to stroke the dog from the side. They should never pat a dog's head, since this is a dominant gesture to a dog.
- Because children are much smaller and less authoritative than adults, they are more at risk from bites.

Adult supervises meeting

◁ **PLAYING SAFE**
Dogs can react nervously to unexpected objects such as this child's skateboard. Keep your dog on a leash in public areas.

Well-trained dog remains calm as girl passes

△ **SNIFF TO INVESTIGATE**
Allow a new dog to sniff and investigate a child only if you are sure the dog is totally reliable, and only in your presence. Teach children that not all dogs are friendly.

HOME ALONE
All dogs, even those with the most affable temperament and generosity of spirit, still have the potential to bite in anger, fear, or pain. Dogs should never be left alone with small children.

61 THE "DOWN & STAY" COMMAND

Teach your dog to stay down on command in order to maintain control in the presence of children or in other distracting environments.

This exercise requires great patience to keep the dog calm at all times. Be careful not to display anger, but also avoid overdoing praise.

1 ◁ With the dog on your left side in the down position (*Tip 48*), give the command "Stay." To reinforce the command, signal with the palm of your left hand toward the dog's face.

Dog watches hand signal

2 ◁ Maintain eye contact with the dog and hold the lead loosely as you walk away. Do not use a food reward, since the dog will want to come to you for it.

3 ▷ Still maintaining eye contact, turn, stand still, and repeat the command "Stay." Gradually extend the duration of the down position.

Leash ensures control

Owner stands up straight to assert authority

4 ◁ Once the dog stays down in your presence, train it to stay down in your absence. Repeat the first three steps, then leave the room. Use a mirror to see if the dog moves.

5 ▷ After several minutes, return to the dog and give the verbal reward "Good dog." You should reward the dog calmly and quietly when it is still lying down. Do not excite the dog, and do not reward it for getting up.

Dog rises up eagerly from down position

6 △ Finally, release the dog from the down position with the word "OK." Don't excite the dog with too much praise – excitement is such a potent reward that the dog will look forward only to the end of the exercise.

AT EASE ▷
This well-trained and obedient Boxer can now be trusted to lie completely relaxed, even in the most distracting environments.

CANINE GAMES

62 STIMULATION THROUGH PLAY

Play constructive games with your dog to provide it with the mental and physical stimulation on which it thrives. It is in a dog's nature to be constantly alert; lack of activity leads to boredom, and bored dogs can be destructive (*Tip 98*). Even the most frivolous games can strengthen the bond between you, and by controlling the games you will reinforce your authority as pack leader.

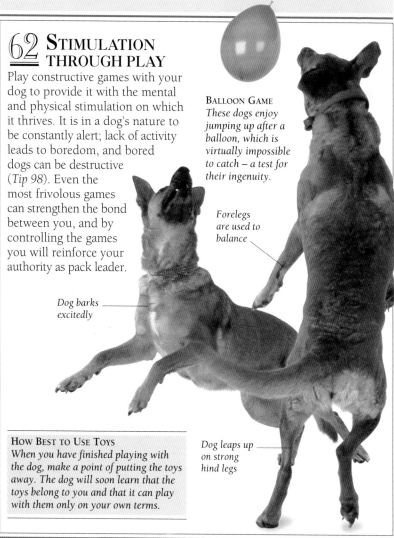

BALLOON GAME
These dogs enjoy jumping up after a balloon, which is virtually impossible to catch – a test for their ingenuity.

Forelegs are used to balance

Dog barks excitedly

HOW BEST TO USE TOYS
When you have finished playing with the dog, make a point of putting the toys away. The dog will soon learn that the toys belong to you and that it can play with them only on your own terms.

Dog leaps up on strong hind legs

63 RETRIEVING GAMES

Catching a toy such as a ball or a Frisbee and returning it is an exciting game for an active, healthy dog. However, note that physically demanding games such as this can be dangerous if your dog is elderly or overweight. Playing retrieving games reinforces your authority because the dog is dependent upon you to throw the toy.

HUNT THE BALL
Chasing games stimulate natural canine behavior. This puppy chases a ball as it would learn to chase its prey in the wild.

Puppy stalks its "prey"

64 HIDE & SEEK

Play hide-and-seek with your dog to test its mental and scenting abilities. Show your dog a favorite toy, then give the command to "Sit and stay" outside a room while you hide the toy (choose a simple hiding place initially). Then allow the dog into the room and tell it to "Fetch" the object. You can use this game as a basis for training your dog to "fetch" a useful item, such as a set of keys, a wallet, or a newspaper – but only on your command.

"SIT & STAY"
Here, the owner gives the command "Sit and stay" before shutting the door and choosing a suitable place to hide a toy.

65 TUG-OF-WAR

Play tug-of-war only when your dog has learned to drop an object on command (*Tip 75*), and always use specially made, robust toys. Do not play this game with dominant or possessive dogs, because they might react aggressively. When you have finished playing the game, make a point of putting the toy away to reestablish that you are the one who is in charge.

PLAYING TO WIN
Most dogs enjoy this stimulating game. But play the game only if you are sure you can win. Some breeds are very powerful.

Toy designed especially for tug-of-war

66 FOLLOWING A SCENT

Lay down a track by walking through grass, leaving a reward such as a toy or a food treat at the end. Scent hounds, such as Beagles and Bloodhounds, particularly relish the mental concentration that is involved following a scent trail. Keep the dog on a leash to keep it from wandering off on the wrong scent trail.

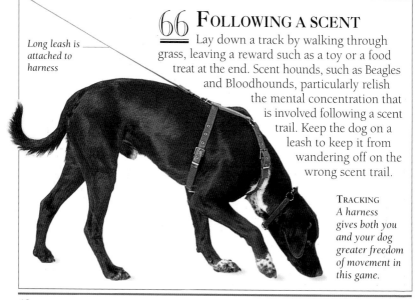

Long leash is attached to harness

TRACKING
A harness gives both you and your dog greater freedom of movement in this game.

67 JOGGING THE DOG

If you enjoy jogging, train your dog to run to heel (*Tip 49*). It will add a new dimension to your exercise routine. The majority of dogs will find this a highly enjoyable "game," although older dogs may tire before their owners do. Some breeds, such as Bulldogs, experience breathing difficulties at the best of times – gentle exercise is better for these dogs.

Dog's tail is erect, indicating excitement

FOLLOW THE LEADER
Healthy and alert, this dog is happy to follow its owner on his morning jog.

Dog follows at owner's heels

68 ACTIVITY GAMES

Train your dog to participate in well-designed activity games. Begin by teaching it to use its paw (*Tip 72*). Many dog clubs hold competitions involving these activities. Retrievers naturally excel at such games.

TOUCH GAME
In this exciting activity game, a "flying mouse" is ejected from a wooden box whenever the dog activates a lever by using its paw.

Dog catches "flying mouse"

Hind legs are bent, ready to spring

ADVANCED TRAINING

69 PROLONGED LIE DOWN

Train your dog to lie down for an extended period to enable you to take it on shopping trips and feel confident that when you tell it to stay, it will be in the same position 20 minutes later.

1 △ Position the dog beside your chair and give the command "Down-stay" (*Tip 61*). Hold on to the dog's leash loosely to enforce the command.

2 △ Each time the dog attempts to leave the down position, say "No" and pull it gently back into position. Repeat the command "Down-stay."

3 ▷ Once the dog lies "flat," it has accepted your command for a prolonged lie down. Twenty minutes later, the dog should still be relaxed.

70 TEACH YOUR DOG TO "SPEAK"

Correct timing is essential when training your dog to bark on command. Tease the dog with a treat, and as soon as you anticipate that it is about to start barking in frustration, give the command "Speak." Reward the dog immediately. Once it understands this command, give the command "Quiet," and offer a treat as soon as the dog stops barking. A barking dog makes an excellent burglar alarm – but you do need an on-off switch.

Alert dog maintains eye contact

Owner stands up straight to help to assert authority

DOG DETERRENT
If you want your dog to bark only as a means of defense against potential attackers, teach the command "Guard" rather than "Speak."

71 DOGS ARE NOT WEAPONS

Train your dog to bark on command to deter criminals, but never teach a dog to attack. Many dogs instinctively defend their human pack's territory, whether it is the car, the home, or the garden.

Teeth bared as warning to potential intruders

DON'T DOCK
Docking tails and clipping ears to make dogs appear more ferocious is censured by most vets and welfare organizations.

72 LEARNING TO TOUCH

Train your dog to use its paw, to teach it dexterity and provide a basis for mentally stimulating games (*Tip 68*). While doing this exercise, prevent your dog from putting its muzzle near the food reward by holding its collar in your left hand.

Dog concentrates on reward hidden in owner's hand

1 △ With the dog on your left side, command it to sit, and kneel down beside it. Show the dog the food that you have concealed in your right hand.

2 △ Push the treat toward the dog's paw. As the dog lifts its paw, move your clenched hand under it and then raise your hand up slightly.

Restrain dog by holding its collar

3 ▷ With the dog's paw resting on your fist, give the command "Paw," then give the dog the food treat. Repeat the exercise, giving praise as a reward.

73 SHAKING HANDS

When your dog has learned to use its paw, simply replace the command "Paw" with "Shake hands." As well as amusing your friends and relations, this valuable exercise reinforces your status as pack leader because, in canine language, raising a paw is a gesture of subservience.

Eye contact asserts your authority

Reward hidden in left hand

74 HOLDING OBJECTS

This exercise is an excellent springboard for retrieving games (*Tip 63*). Tease the dog with a suitable object – a rolled-up newspaper is perfect. Hold the dog's head up, making sure the dog is not uncomfortable, and gently place the object into its mouth. Give the command "Hold."

DON'T FEED THE DOG
With this exercise, you must give only verbal or physical praise: a dog will drop the object if shown a food treat.

SHOP ASSISTANT
This Labrador is always happy to carry its owner's newspaper home from the store.

75 RETRIEVING OBJECTS

Once your dog has learned to pick up and hold an object (*Tip 74*), teach it to chase and retrieve. This exercise stimulates the dog's natural instinct to pursue its prey.

Retrieving is an especially useful skill for active dogs such as gun dogs and terriers – since it enables you to exercise the dog thoroughly without exhausting yourself.

1 ◁ Use a leash to enforce your commands at first. Hold the dog by its collar with one hand and throw a favorite toy with your free hand.

PUP RETRIEVERS
If you are training a puppy, then use a squeaky toy and let the puppy play with it. Praise the pup when it drops the toy naturally.

2 ◁ Command the dog to "Fetch" as you release your grip on its collar. Having been trained to pick up and hold the toy, the dog should now chase it eagerly.

3 ◁ Once the dog has picked up the object, crouch or kneel down and give the command "Come" to recall it.

Owner rewards dog with praise and strokes

4 △ Say "Good dog" and issue the command "Give" as you take the toy from the dog's mouth. As soon as the dog releases the object, repeat the verbal praise "Good dog."

5 ◁ To remind the dog that you are still in control, give the command "Sit." After a few successful training sessions, repeat the exercise without the leash.

Dog waits for owner to repeat the "game"

76 RELUCTANT RETRIEVERS

If your dog is unwilling to fetch an object you have thrown, make the exercise more interesting by using a squeaky toy and running with the dog on its leash to where you have thrown the object.

- If the dog reaches the toy and looks puzzled, it has not learned to hold properly (*Tip 74*).
- If the dog picks up the toy but does not return it, go back to recall training (*Tip 46*).

77 FETCHING FROM WATER

Most dogs are fine swimmers: avoid treacherous or icy waters, however.

- Be wary of water-borne diseases, such as leptospirosis and blue-green algal bloom, which can cause itchy skin, diarrhea, or even death.
- Make sure that your dog is able to get out of a body of water safely.

EAGERLY IN THE SWIM

RETRAINING

78 WHEN IS RETRAINING NECESSARY?

Rescued dogs, especially mature ones, often arrive with unexpected behavioral problems. However, even the most obedient pet can develop unwanted habits at some stage.

Old dog still has alert expression

KEEPING BUSY ▷
Tail chasing is self-rewarding behavior that should be discouraged.

◁ **OLD TIMER**
Although set in their ways, older dogs may still be successfully retrained with patience.

PATIENT RETRAINING
Slow, repetitive, and consistent training is required to remedy ingrained behavioral problems.

79 NERVOUS DOGS

Fear of strangers, loud noises, children, uniforms, or any living or inanimate object may occur in any dog, often as a consequence of restricted early learning. Reduce nervousness by initially avoiding the causes, if at all possible. Then, over a period of a few weeks, gradually expose the dog to situations that make it nervous. Reward calm behavior with soothing words.

SEEKING SHELTER

80 ASSESSING TEMPERAMENT

When choosing a dog from a shelter, be sure to assess the dog's temperament, rather than simply judging it on its looks. Check for behavioral problems using a few simple tests. Take the dog only if it responds well to the tests, or if you are sure that you have the amount of time and patience required to deal with problems that are evident.

FEAR OF HANDS ▽
Stroke the dog under its chin, and then down its back. Talk to the dog calmly as you do this. A dog that fears hands will pull away.

◁ **TEST OF NERVE**
With a handler from the shelter holding the dog on a leash, quietly approach the dog. A nervous dog may bark or cower.

Stand upright and establish eye contact

Dog accepts being touched

CREATIVE TESTING
Some dogs are scared of loud noises; others are scared of children. Try to test the dog in the everyday situations it is likely to encounter in your home.

TESTING OBEDIENCE ▷
Command the dog to sit. Its response will tell you whether it has had any training. If the dog does not obey, tuck it into a sit position, to gauge its response to training.

81 FEAR OF STRANGERS

Although you will have an idea of the dog's temperament from your own first encounter with it (*Tip 80*), it is worthwhile to have the dog examined by a stranger. This will indicate any problems that might appear on visits to the vet. A dog that is wary of strangers will display obvious signs of its discomfort, such as violent trembling or cowering, and it may even attempt to bite from fear (*Tip 83*).

Stranger approaches cautiously

This dog shows no signs of fear

82 FEAR OF DOGS

With the help of the handler, introduce the dog to a confident dog of the same sex. If the dog simply sniffs the new arrival curiously, there should be no problems with aggression toward other dogs.

Dogs greet each other confidently

83 FEAR BITING

The fear-biting dog is more apprehensive than an aggressive animal. The problem often results from inadequate socialization. Retraining is slow and cautious, best done with professional help.

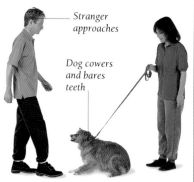

Stranger approaches

Dog cowers and bares teeth

84 TWO'S A CROWD

If you already have a dog, take care when introducing another. Remember that your dog is more likely to tolerate the presence of a dog of the opposite sex. The initial meeting should take place with both dogs on a leash. Place food bowls so the dogs face in opposite directions.

Possessive dog snaps at interloper to guard its toy

WHAT'S YOURS IS MINE
Most dogs want what another dog has; do not expect your dog to share its toys with a new arrival.

85 INTRODUCING A NEW PUPPY

A new puppy is a potential threat to the territory of the resident dog. Do not let the pup jump on the older dog: the resident dog will find this provocative. Arrange meetings when both animals are relaxed, and reward the dog for its obedience in the presence of the newcomer.
- Continue to greet and reward the resident dog before the newcomer.
- Provide each dog with its own bed, placed in its own private area.

CLOSE ENCOUNTER OF THE FURRED KIND
Ideally, keep the puppy in its crate when introducing the older dog. The resident dog will be able to investigate the new arrival without fear of harassment.

BEHAVIORAL PROBLEMS

86 PREVENTING PROBLEMS

Obedience training from an early age is the best way to prevent canine behavioral problems, and prevention is better and easier than cure. Seek professional help if you are unable to train your dog; never resort to physical violence.

- Discipline your dog only when it is actively misbehaving. It must know why it is being punished.
- Remember that a dog does not misbehave to punish its owner: retribution is a fault in humans, but not in dogs.

Dog does not know that it has done anything wrong

DESTRUCTIVE CHEWING
Separation anxiety can lead to behavioral problems such as destructive chewing or digging.

Lonesome dog is apt to chew any item left lying around

87 CHASING VEHICLES

The sight of a cyclist can stimulate a dog to give chase: it's an instinctive reaction. To deal with this problem, ask a friend to cycle past the dog. As it begins to chase, the cyclist should stop and squirt the dog with a water pistol, and say "No" in a stern voice.

DOG HAZARD
Chasing is a bad problem that can cause serious accidents.

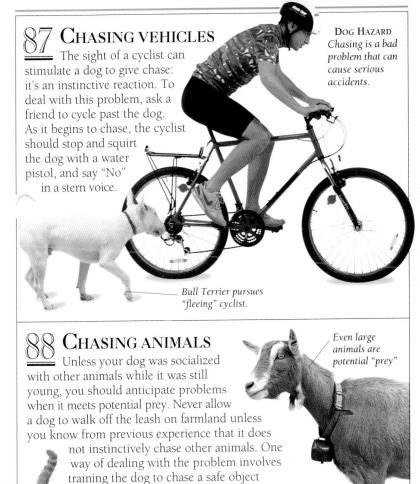

Bull Terrier pursues "fleeing" cyclist.

88 CHASING ANIMALS

Unless your dog was socialized with other animals while it was still young, you should anticipate problems when it meets potential prey. Never allow a dog to walk off the leash on farmland unless you know from previous experience that it does not instinctively chase other animals. One way of dealing with the problem involves training the dog to chase a safe object instead of other animals (*Tip 75*).

Even large animals are potential "prey"

◁ **DOMESTIC PROBLEM**
Other domestic pets may be seen as prey to a dog that has not been socialized.

FARMYARD THREAT ▷
Instinctive hunters, dogs will chase farm animals such as sheep and goats.

89 AGGRESSIVE BEHAVIOR

Most dogs are content to be treated as subordinate members of the pack and are willing to obey the commands of their human family. Some dogs, however, are unwittingly taught by their owners that they are the pack leaders. They are allowed to go through doors first, are fed first, and are given affection on demand. Once a dog thinks it is pack leader, it is likely to use aggression to enforce its control. You may well require the services of a professional dog trainer to remedy this behavior.

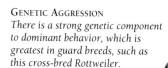

GENETIC AGGRESSION
There is a strong genetic component to dominant behavior, which is greatest in guard breeds, such as this cross-bred Rottweiler.

90 TIGHT-LEASH SYNDROME

Some dogs will aggressively defend their owners. Standing between you and the other dog (or approaching stranger) and pulling on the leash actually enhances the dog's feeling of aggression. Although you may instinctively keep the dog on a short leash when it shows aggression, this will often exacerbate the situation. Turn your dog's head away so that it cannot make eye contact with the other dog.

ACT QUICKLY
You should intervene the moment that your dog makes eye contact with a potential adversary. A raised tail and intense concentration are indicators that a fight might begin.

91 REMEDIES FOR AGGRESSION

An aggressive dog must be taught that you, and not it, are the pack leader. In canine society, leaders eat first and have demands for affection met immediately. Make sure that your dominant dog is last to eat, and teach it that it must be obedient to earn your affection.

- Groom a dominant dog at least once a day, making sure it is muzzled and wearing a houseline.
- If necessary, seek professional help.

Owner ignores dog's attention seeking

Restrained dog obeys "Sit" command

REDUCING RISKS △
Use a muzzle or adjustable head collar while encouraging the dog to respond to commands. This will reduce the risk of bites during remedial training.

Dog obeys owner's firm command

WITHDRAW AFFECTION △
Disregard the dog until it stops making demands, then order it to sit, and stroke it. Show it that you are in control.

NO LUXURIES ▷
Making sure that the dog wears a houseline at home, give the command "Off" if it climbs on furniture.

92 POSSESSIVENESS

Avoid confrontation with a possessive dog by not giving it toys and not allowing it to sit on the furniture. Treat problems by withdrawing affection, reteaching basic commands, and keeping your dog on a long training leash until it remembers who is the boss.

PERSONAL SPACE
This terrier becomes aggressive when ordered off the bed, which it considers its personal space.

93 SEXUAL MISBEHAVIOR

If your dog habitually attempts to mount your leg or the legs of visitors, keep it on a leash or houseline so that you can pull it away. Say "No" firmly, and isolate the dog for a minute or two. Allow the dog back into your company, but ignore it for another few minutes. Then, tell it to sit, give it a reward, and play with it. The fact that the dog has tried to mount your leg indicates its need for physical and mental stimulation.

MOUNTING PROBLEMS
Overexcited by seeing its owner, this Golden Retriever attempts to mount his leg. Note: bitches will also indulge in this activity.

94 JUMPING UP

Although jumping up is a natural play activity among dogs, it is potentially dangerous to people. Jumping usually occurs when the dog is excited by seeing its owner or visitors arrive at the house. Ignore the greeting and, avoiding eye contact, walk past the dog. When the dog's feet are back on the ground, tell it to sit, then get down to its level and praise its obedience.

Leonberger stretches to lick owner's face

Dog stands on hind legs

WELCOME HOME
This Leonberger jumps up to greet its owner, just as it jumped up to greet his mother as a puppy. It is very dangerous behavior from such a massive dog.

Owner avoids eye contact

95 ATTENTION SEEKING

Some breeds – small ones in particular – jump up, bark, scratch, or lick in order to attract attention or beg for food. This is canine bad manners, and you should not allow your dog to do this. Never feed the dog from the table, and do not respond to its demands, no matter how tempting it may be to do so. You should try to reduce the dog's dependence on you by making sure that other members of your family, as well as friends, play with it and feed it.

DEPENDENT DOG
This overly dependent dog persistently scratches to seek its owner's attention – a common problem with smaller dogs.

96 PROBLEMS IN CARS

Some dogs dislike traveling in cars because of the uncontrolled motion, resulting in nausea. If your dog experiences car sickness, don't feed it before a trip, and protect the car with newspaper and old towels.

- Reprimand your dog if it defends the car as its own personal territory.
- Muzzle the dog to help prevent destructive behavior in your car.

PERSISTENT BARKING △
If the dog barks excessively on car trips, someone should sit with it and command it to be quiet when necessary.

DIGGING UPHOLSTERY △
If your dog chews the car interior, treat the upholstery with a bitter spray (Tip 53) and provide the dog with a chew toy.

SUNBLIND △
As well as keeping the sun off the dog, a sunblind can help calm excitable dogs by obscuring the view that stimulates them.

PROVIDE REFRESHMENT
Make sure that you have a container of water in the car, especially on long trips. You should stop every few hours to allow the dog to drink and relieve itself.

DISCOURAGE DESTRUCTIVE BEHAVIOR
If your dog is crate trained (Tip 41), then using a travel crate will offer safety and eliminate any destructive activity.

CANINE SEATBELTS
Specially designed seatbelts will limit the dog's movement, prevent it from distracting the driver, and can reduce the risk of injury in an accident.

97 HOWLING

Left alone, a nervous dog may bark or howl. This is particularly common in dogs that have not been properly socialized as puppies or have known several homes. Before leaving your house, provide the dog with a special treat, such as a favorite chew toy that you have rubbed in your hands.

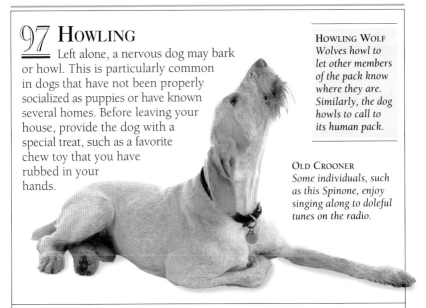

HOWLING WOLF
Wolves howl to let other members of the pack know where they are. Similarly, the dog howls to call to its human pack.

OLD CROONER
Some individuals, such as this Spinone, enjoy singing along to doleful tunes on the radio.

98 BOREDOM

Dogs do not like being alone. They are a sociable species, and it is unnatural for them not to have companionship or activity. Most bored dogs just look glum and lie around, but many grow destructive. Always anticipate your pet's needs and create mentally and physically demanding activities for it. Ideally, provide a playmate for your dog.

DOG'S LIFE
Mental stimulation would transform the gloomy aspect of this Golden Retriever.

99 DIGGING UP TROUBLE

While some dogs dig to bury bones, and others to create cool pits in which to lie, many dig in an attempt to escape confinement or out of sheer frustration at being left alone. Digging provides a natural mental and physical activity for dogs. In order to discourage digging, you must provide alternative outlets for your dog's industriousness.

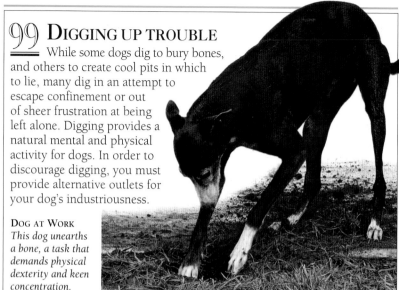

DOG AT WORK
This dog unearths a bone, a task that demands physical dexterity and keen concentration.

100 SEEKING PROFESSIONAL HELP

Some serious problems, such as fear biting (*Tip 83*), warrant the assistance of a personal trainer. Your vet should be able to suggest someone to help. Even if your dog is obedient, it is worth considering advanced training classes. Advanced training will help cultivate the full potential of the partnership between you and your canine companion.

BACK TO BASICS
If you do have to correct bad behavior, it will be much easier if your dog has already been taught basic obedience.

FINE TUNING
Advanced training classes can introduce both you and your dog to the enjoyment of canine activity games.

101 YOU & YOUR DOG

Answer the questions set out below by checking the relevant box. If your answers are mainly in the first column, you are well on your way to effective dog training. If most of your answers are in the second column, seek professional advice from an experienced handler.

Training Record

Where did you buy your dog?		Breeder/friend	Shelter/pet shop
How old was your new pet?		Under 26 weeks	Over 26 weeks
Is your male dog neutered?		Yes	No
Is your dog a guarding breed?		No	Yes
Is it your first dog?		No	Yes
When is your dog fed?		At set times	On demand
Does your dog eat after you?		Yes	No
Where does your dog sleep?		Kitchen/outside	Bedroom/on bed
When is your dog groomed?		Frequently	Infrequently
When is your dog exercised?		At set times	On demand
How long is the exercise period?		Over 1 hour/day	Under 1 hour/day
When does your dog eliminate?		At set times	On demand
Where are the dog's toys kept?		In toy container	On floor
Does your dog have a playmate?		Yes	No
Does your dog meet strangers?		Frequently	Infrequently
Is your dog often left alone?		No	Yes
Do you have off-leash control?		Yes	No

OBEDIENT COMPANION
This well-trained poodle is happy to lie still for prolonged periods (Tip 69).

INDEX

Acknowledgments

Dorling Kindersley would like to thank Hilary Bird for compiling the index, Fiona Wild for proofreading and editorial help, Robert Campbell and Mark Bracey for DTP assistance, and Caroline Potts for picture research.

Photography
KEY: t *top*; b *bottom*; c *center*; l *left*; r *right*
All photographs by Tim Ridley, Steve Gorton, and Andy Crawford except for: Jane Burton 6t, 12b, 61br; Nicholas Goodhall 56tr, 61t; Dave King 8, 10t, 11b, 14, 16t; Tracy Morgan Animal Photography 10b, 11t, m, 13b, 16b, 18r, 28cb, 29tl, tr, 31t, b, 32t, 33t, 35, 36, 37t, bl, 38t, 40t, 43b, 51, 53b, 59b, 68b; Damien Moore 2, 37br; David Ward 3, 7b, 9b, 12tl, 13t, 15b, 17b, 42b, 46, 56b, 59t, 60, 61bl, 64, 65t, 66, 67, 68t, 69, 72